Poetry

And Then There Were Eight

Poems about Space

Revised Edition

by Laura Purdie Salas

T0044777

CAPSTONE PRESS
a capstone imprint

The View

Earthrise
fills the skies
across the void
of space
it lies

Sky delight
blue and bright
shining in the
secret
night

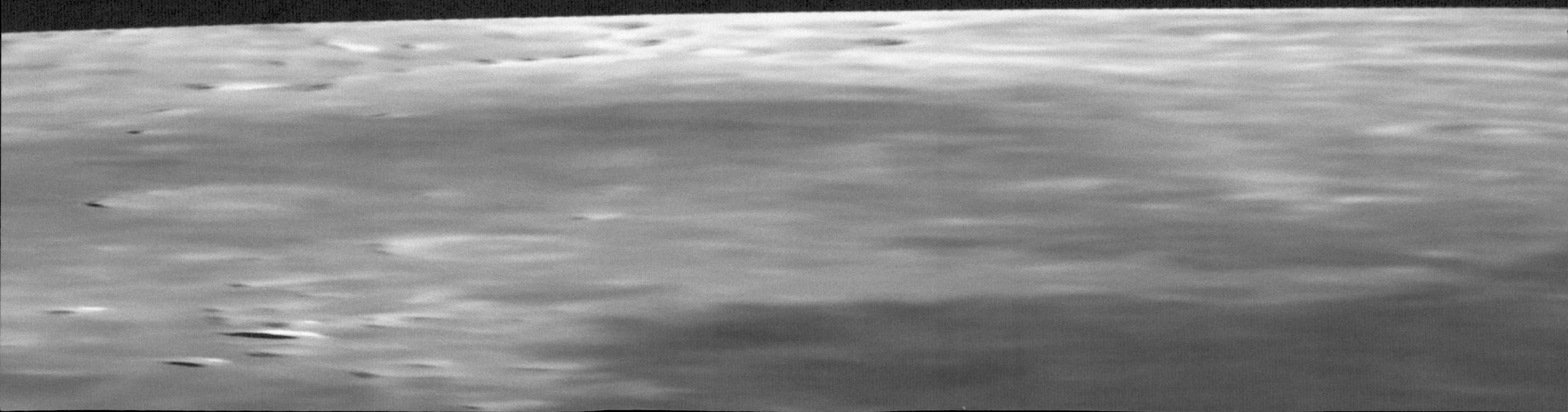

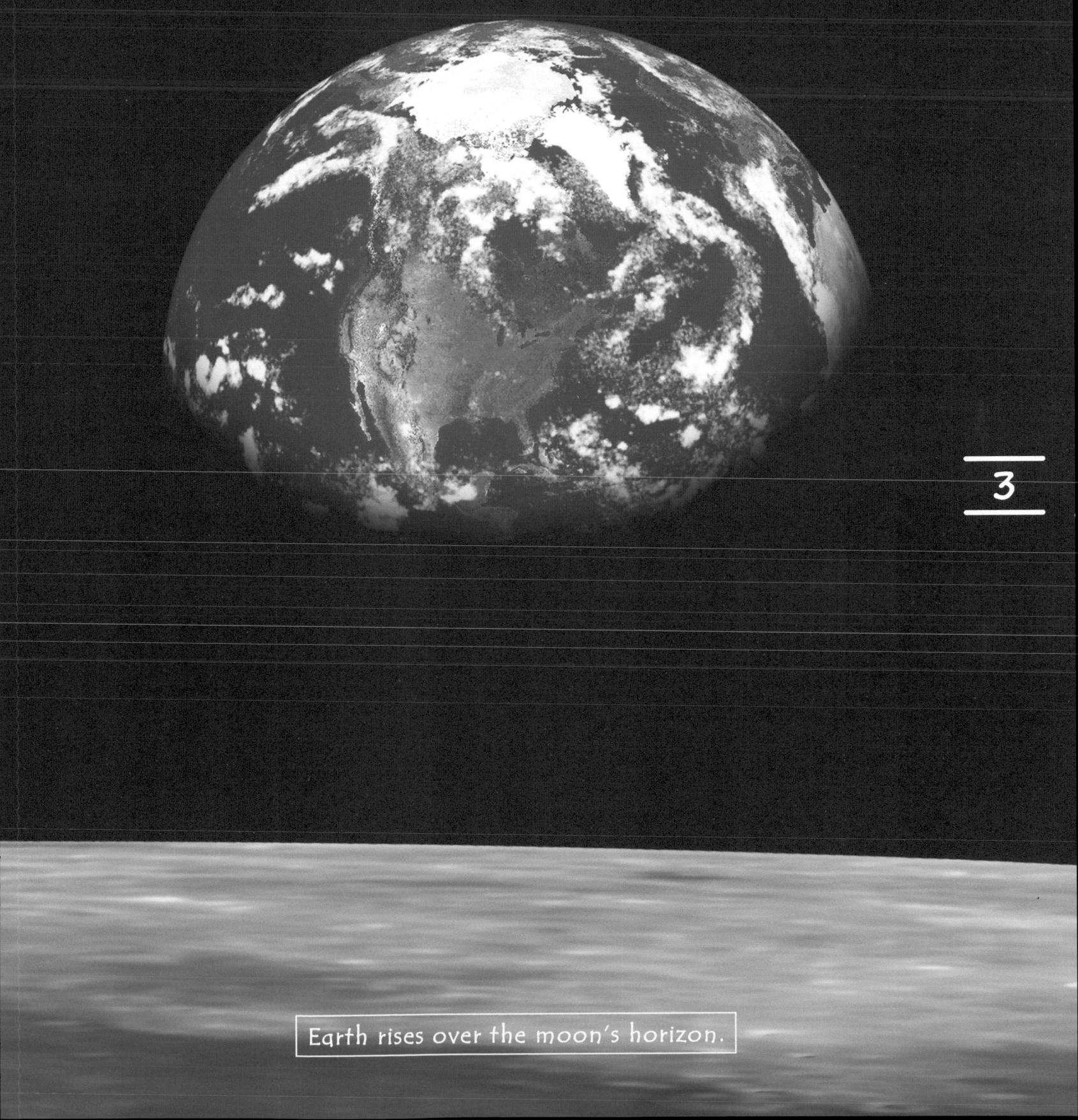

Earth rises over the moon's horizon.

3-2-1

Waiting's over, sky is clear
Counting down now, launch is near!
Shuttle points toward deep black space
Giant step for human race
Trailing smoke clouds flaming hot —

I wish I were an astronaut!

Lost in Space

5

There once was a man on the moon
Who let go of his birthday balloon
"It's drifting away!"
He cried in dismay
And he looked for it all afternoon

Sky Eye

I like to look
into the sky,
a sea
of velvet black

But just last night
I realized
the sky
was looking back!

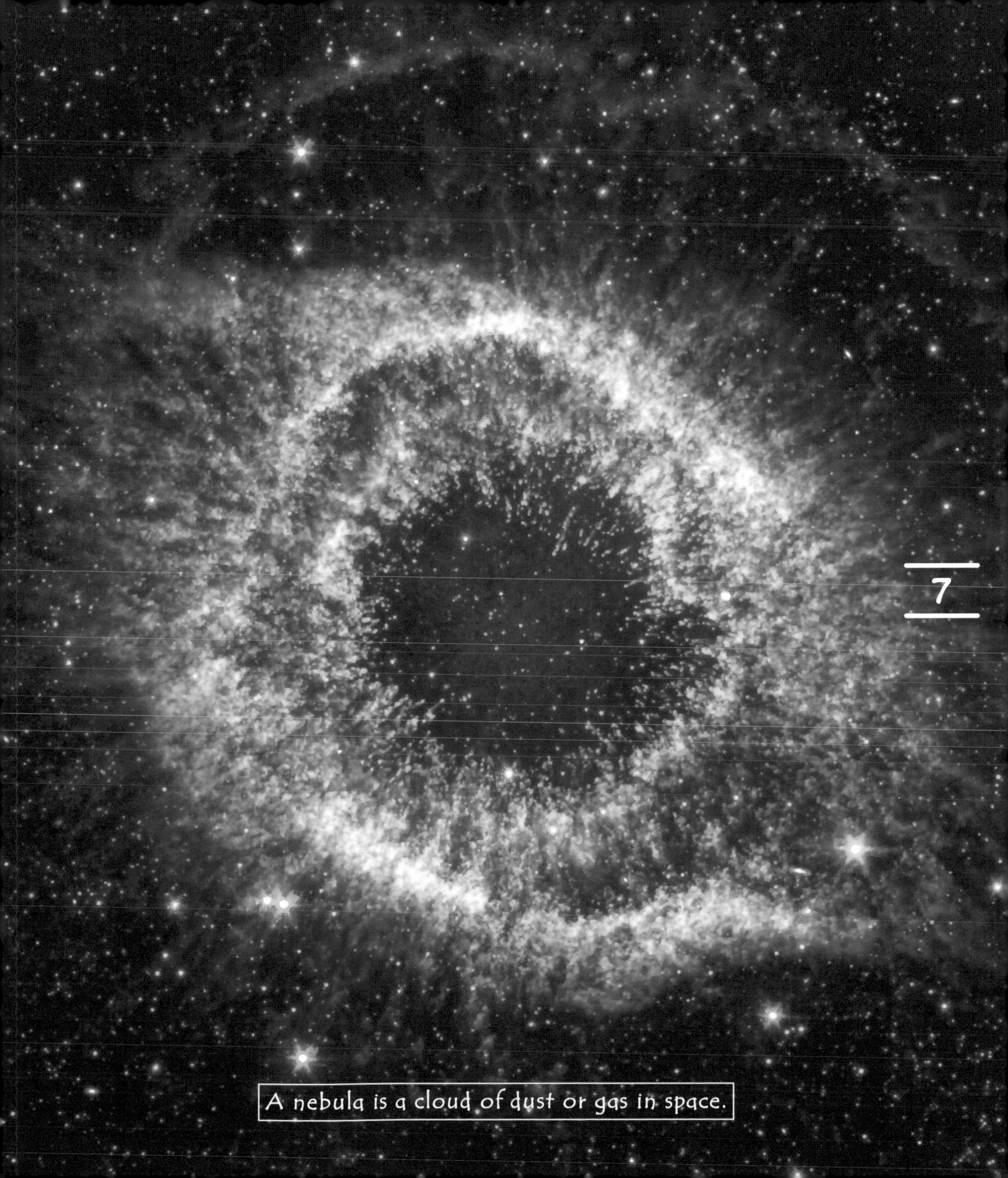

A nebula is a cloud of dust or gas in space.

Great Red Spot

It's not a huge red ocean
It's not a desert form
It's twice as big as Planet Earth
And it's a great red storm

It's been around three hundred years
It's still around today
According to the weatherman
This storm is here to stay

(at least until some future day
still centuries away!)

The Great Red Spot on Jupiter is actually a giant hurricane.

Moon
dances
a graceful ballet
around Earth
It decorates the
stage of sky,
shining in a spotlight of
sun

Ballerina

The Moon glows because the Sun's light bounces off of it.

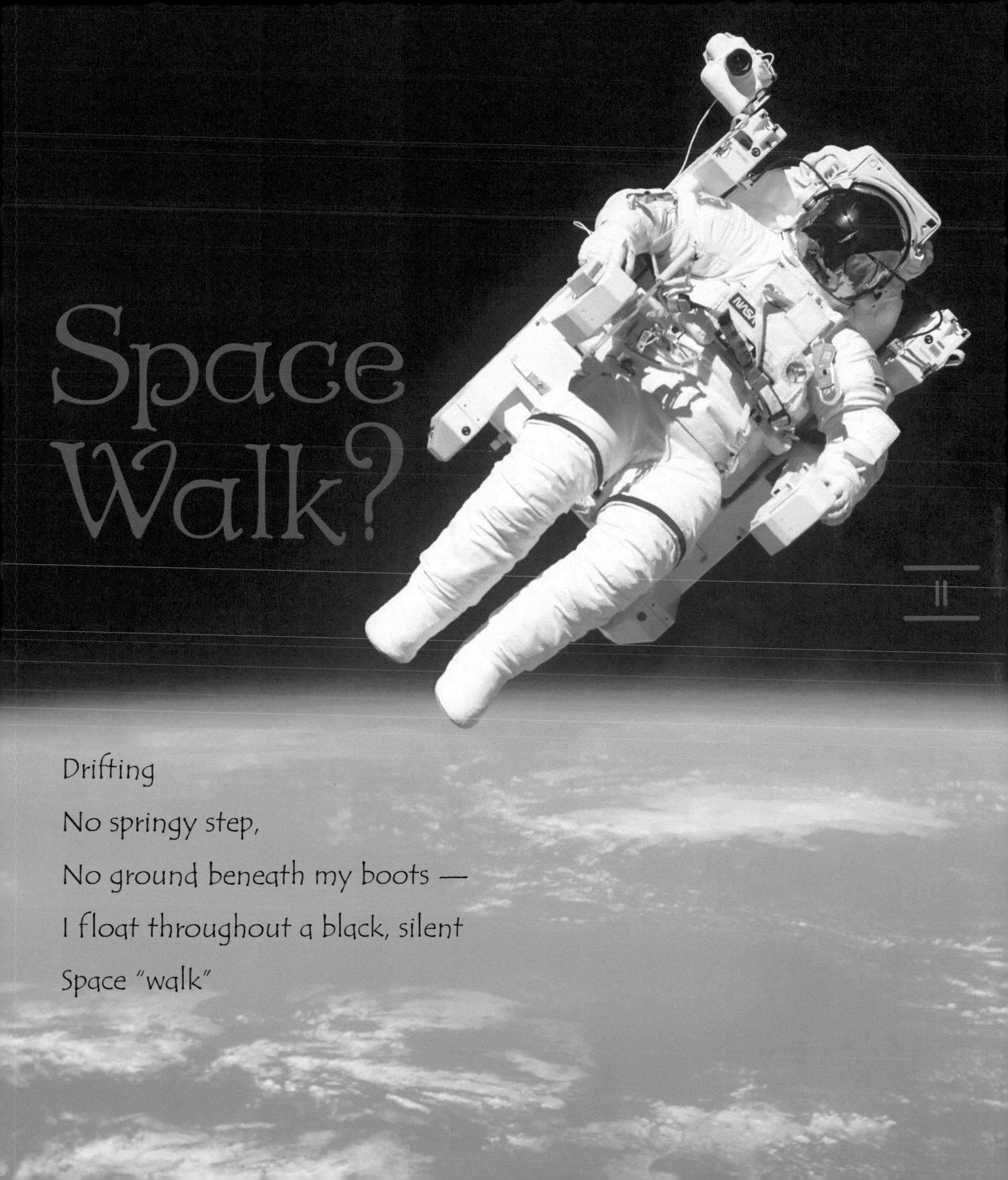

Drifting
No springy step,
No ground beneath my boots —
I float throughout a black, silent
Space "walk"

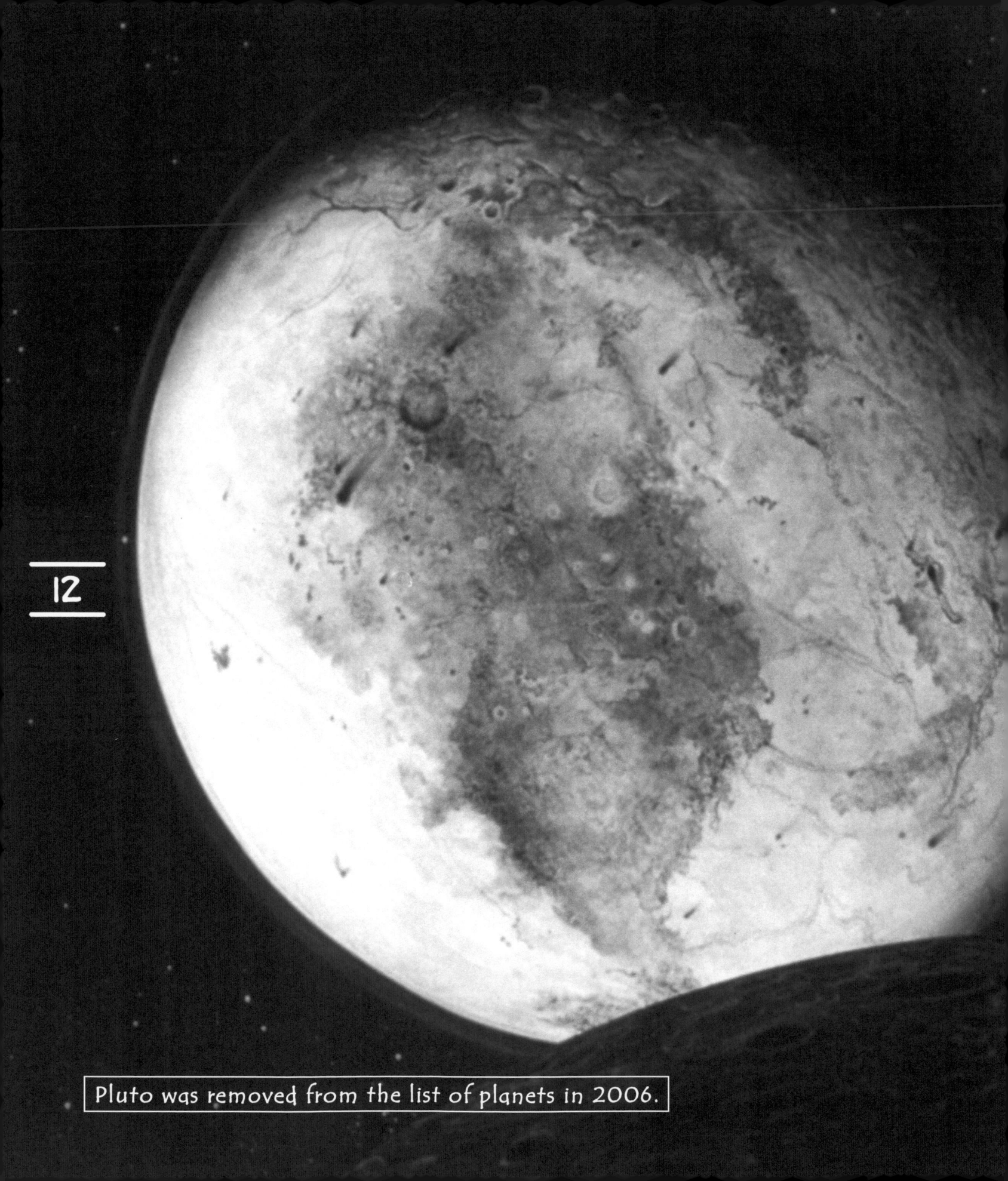

Pluto was removed from the list of planets in 2006.

Then There Were Eight

Poor ball of ice, we know you exist; but you're
Little and solid and we must insist on
Undoing the past, so though you'll be missed, we've
Taken you
Off of the "real planet" list

Aiming High

Silver arrow to the skies, you're my mighty mirrored eyes
Finding stars and Saturn's bands, you place them gently in my hands

A telescope uses mirrors and light to make faraway objects appear closer.

On the Moon

No rains fall
No winds gust
A human footprint
Fixed in dust

Hours on hours
Days on days
Our magic landing
Stays and stays

An astronaut left this footprint on the moon in 1969.
The moon has no wind or rain to erase the footprint.

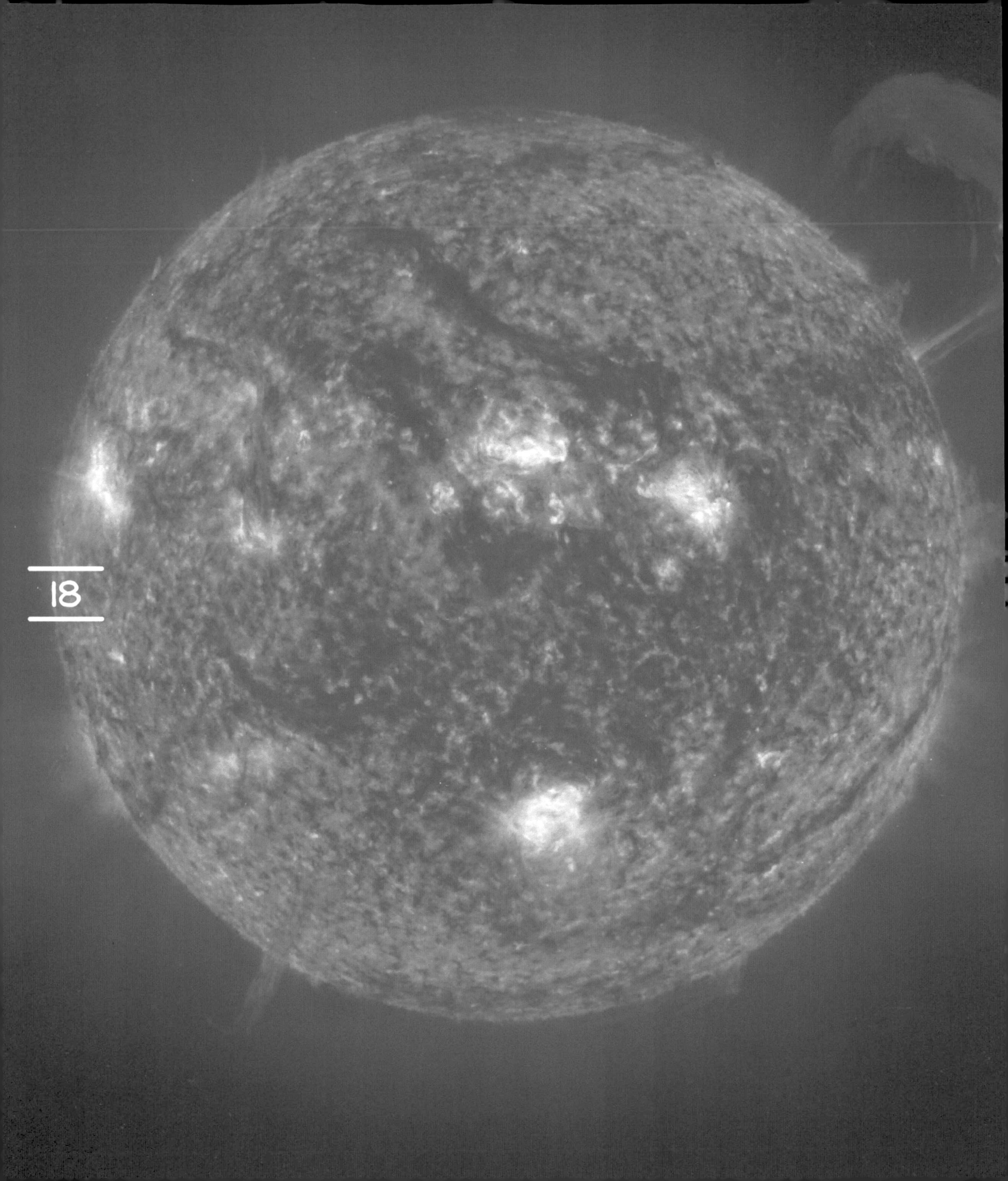
18

Just Right

Sun

We love you

Yes

We need you

You

Bring warmth and life and light

Come

Too close and

We

Would burn up

Go

And it's eternal night

Saturn

Saturn's
giant
Saturn's
gas
No solid
ground for
trees or grass

Saturn's
banded
Saturn
swings
A skirt of
circling
rocky rings

A Greek myth says that when a hunter chased seven sisters, Zeus changed the girls into doves. They flew to the sky and became stars.

Family Flock

Seven sisters, lovely, kind
Daughters of the sky and sea
Greedy hunter close behind
How can they stay wild and free?

Each becomes a snow-white dove
That flies up high to join the night
A brilliant flock of sister love
Soaring in forever flight

Here, Girl!

She rolls

and roams

and wags her tail

She never needs to see the vet

I love her

silver

shiny coat

She's my planetary pet!

The Mars Lander explores Mars.

Magic

fuschia and lime green
lights slide down night's northern sky —

winter's magic show

Energy from the sun causes northern lights to appear near the Arctic Circle.

The Language of Poetry

Couplet two lines that end with words that rhyme

Repetition the use of a word or phrase more than one time

Rhyme to have an end sound that is the same as the end sound of another word

Rhythm the pattern of beats in a poem

Acrostic

The subject of the poem is written straight down the page. Each line of the poem starts with a letter from the word. "Then There Were Eight" (page 13) is an acrostic poem.

Cinquain

A poem with five lines. The first line has two syllables. The second line has four, the third has six, the fourth has eight, and the last line has two syllables. "Space Walk?" (page 11) is an example of a cinquain.

Free Verse

A poem that does not follow a set pattern or rhythm. It often does not rhyme. "Ballerina" (page 10) is an example of free verse.

Haiku

A short poem that describes a scene in nature. It has five syllables in the first line, seven syllables in the second line, and five syllables in the third line. "Magic" (page 27) is an example of a haiku.

Limerick

A five-line poem that follows a certain rhythm. The first, second, and fifth lines rhyme, and so do the third and fourth lines. "Lost in Space " (page 5) is a limerick.

Glossary

astronaut (ASS-truh-nawt) — someone who travels in space

banded (BAND-id) — striped

brilliant (BRIL-yuhnt) — shining very brightly

century (SEN-chuh-ree) — a period of 100 years

dismay (diss-MAY) — worry

earthrise (URTH-rize) — the Earth appearing in the sky; an earthrise is seen from outer space.

eternal (i-TUR-nuhl) — lasting forever

fuschia (FEW-shah) — a dark purplish-red color

launch (LAWNCH) — to send a rocket up into space

void (VOID) — an empty space

Read More

Florian, Douglas. *Comets, Stars, the Moon, and Mars: Space Poems and Paintings*. Orlando, Fla.: Harcourt, 2007.

Foster, John, editor. *Space Poems*. New York: Oxford University Press, 2008.

Internet Sites

Facthound offers a safe, fun way to find Internet sites related to this book. All of the sites on FactHound have been researched by our staff.

Here's how:

1. Visit *www.facthound.com*

2. Choose your grade level.

3. Type in this book ID **142961207X** for age-appropriate sites. You may also browse subjects by clicking on letters, or by clicking on pictures and words.

4. Click on the **Fetch It** button.

FactHound will fetch the best sites for you!

Index of Poems

3-2-1, 4

Aiming High, 14

Ballerina, 10

Family Flock, 23

Great Red Spot, 8

Here, Girl!, 24

Just Right, 19

Lost in Space, 5

Magic, 27

On the Moon, 16

Saturn, 20

Sky Eye, 6

Space Walk?, 11

Then There Were Eight, 13

View, The, 2

A+ Books are published by Capstone Press,
1710 Roe Crest Drive, North Mankato, Minnesota 56003.
www.mycapstone.com

Copyright © 2008, 2016 Capstone Press, a Capstone imprint. All rights reserved.
No part of this publication may be reproduced in whole or in part, or stored in a retrieval system, or transmitted in any form or by any means, electronic, mechanical, photocopying, recording, or otherwise, without written permission of the publisher.
For information regarding permission, write to Capstone Press,
1710 Roe Crest Drive, North Mankato, Minnesota 56003.

Library of Congress Cataloging-in-Publication Data is available on the Library of Congress Website

ISBN: 978-1-5157-6153-2 (revised paperback)
ISBN: 978-1-5157-6154-9 (ebook pdf)

Credits
Jenny Marks, editor; Ted Williams, designer; Scott Thoms, photo researcher

Photo Credits
iStockphoto: Lars Lentz, 20-21
NASA: 12, 16-17, JPL-Caltech, 7, 25, JPL/ESA, 18, JPL/University of Arizona, 8-9, JSC, 5, 10, KSC, 4
Shutterstock: Anastasiya Igolkina, Cover, 1, 28, David W. Kelley, 11, Kanuman, 26-27, Knud Nielsen, 15, Paul LeFevre, 22-23, Stasys Eidiejus, 2-3

Note to Parents, Teachers, and Librarians
And Then There Were Eight: Poems about Space uses colorful photographs and a nonfiction format to introduce children to poetry and outer space themes. This book is designed to be read independently by an early reader or to be read aloud to a pre-reader. The images help early readers and listeners understand the poems and concepts discussed. The book encourages further learning by including the following sections: The Language of Poetry, Glossary, Read More, Internet Sites, and Index. Early readers may need assistance using these features.

Printed in the United States 4755